NBA

UNDERDOG STORIES

BY MARTY GITLIN

UNDERDOG SPORTS STORIES

SportsZone

An Imprint of Abdo Publishing | abdobooks.com

abdobooks.com

Published by Abdo Publishing, a division of ABDO, PO Box 398166, Minneapolis, Minnesota 55439.

Printed in the United States of America, North Mankato, Minnesota
092018
012019

THIS BOOK CONTAINS RECYCLED MATERIALS

Cover Photo: Frank Gunn/The Canadian Press/AP Images
Interior Photos: AP Images, 5, 6; M. Spencer Green/AP Images, 8; Stephen Dunn/Getty Images Sport/Getty Images, 11; North Carolina State University/Collegiate Images/Getty Images, 12; Bettmann/Getty Images, 15; Gary Stewart/AP Images, 17, 18, 21; Duane Burleson/AP Images, 23; Mark Duncan/AP Images, 24; Paul Sancya/AP Images, 26; Jeff Chiu/AP Images, 29, 30; Marcio Jose Sanchez/AP Images, 33; Elise Amendola/AP Images, 35; Bill Kostroun/AP Images, 36, 41; Pat Sullivan/AP Images, 38; Tony Dejak/AP Images, 42; Lukas Schulze/picture-alliance/dpa/AP Images, 45

Editor: Patrick Donnelly
Series Designer: Melissa Martin

Library of Congress Control Number: 2018949195

Publisher's Cataloging-in-Publication Data

Names: Gitlin, Marty, author.
Title: NBA underdog stories / by Marty Gitlin.
Description: Minneapolis, Minnesota : Abdo Publishing, 2019 | Series: Underdog sports stories | Includes online resources and index.
Identifiers: ISBN 9781532117626 (lib. bdg.) | ISBN 9781532170485 (ebook)
Subjects: LCSH: Basketball--Juvenile literature. | National Basketball Association--Juvenile literature. | Upsets in sports--Juvenile literature. | Winning and losing--Juvenile literature.
Classification: DDC 796.32364--dc23

TABLE OF CONTENTS

CHAPTER 1

A LOVE STORY

The greatest victories in sports are not always reflected on a scoreboard at the end of a game. Some are earned by overcoming major obstacles along the way.

One such triumph was achieved by Bob Love. The early 1970s National Basketball Association (NBA) standout cleared two major hurdles to emerge as one of the finest forwards of his generation. Love excelled despite a stutter that hampered his communication with teammates.

Bob Love broke into the NBA with the Cincinnati Royals in 1966.

ROYALS

And he was a fourth-round draft pick—not the résumé you'd expect from a three-time All-Star.

Love was an underdog throughout his life. He grew up dirt poor in the small town of Bastrop, Louisiana. His classmates teased him for his stuttering. He often came home crying. But he gained inspiration from his grandmother. She told him that he could achieve anything if he believed in himself and chased his dreams.

Love carried that advice with him forever. The dream he pursued was to become a sports star. He worked hard.

Love is honored after scoring his 10,000th career point in 1974.

He developed his talents as a quarterback as well. And soon he was leading his Morehouse High School football and basketball teams to state championships.

Love earned a football scholarship to Southern University in Louisiana. But he gave up the sport because he believed he was too skinny to face college defenses. He felt safer playing basketball. It turned out to be a great decision. Love blossomed on the court and shattered school scoring records. He averaged 25.6 points per game as a junior and 30.6 as a senior.

NBA scouts tend to ignore players from small schools, so Love had to wait until the fourth round of the 1965 draft before he was selected by the Cincinnati Royals. He didn't get much playing time in his first two seasons. The Milwaukee Bucks acquired Love during an expansion draft before his third season. But just 14 games into that season, the Bucks traded him to the Chicago Bulls.

The Bulls benefited from their faith in Love. He averaged 20 points per game in his first full season with Chicago. He matched or exceeded that total in each of the next five years. Love was twice named to the All-NBA team and earned a spot on the All-Defensive team three times.

Love overcame his speech impediment to become an accomplished public speaker.

He finished his career as the leading scorer in Bulls history. Only the legendary Michael Jordan and Scottie Pippen have since passed him.

Still, the stuttering problem persisted throughout his career. But Love refused to give in. Extensive speech therapy helped him conquer his stuttering. This helped him when he ran for public office in Chicago. He even became a motivational speaker. Eventually Love landed a job as the Bulls' Director of Community Affairs. The career required plenty of speaking. But Love embraced the words of his grandmother. He knew he could accomplish anything if he worked hard and believed in himself.

A STRANGE NICKNAME

Bob Love was known as "Butterbean" because he enjoyed butterbeans growing up in rural Louisiana. A butterbean is what lima beans are often called in the southern part of the United States.

CHAPTER 2

SUPER SPUD

On February 8, 1986, fans at Reunion Arena in Dallas were in for a rare treat. Hometown hero Spud Webb was competing in the finals of the NBA Slam Dunk Contest. That's a big deal for any player, but especially for one who stood just 5 feet 6 inches tall.

Webb looked like a sapling in a forest of redwoods. His opponent for the crown was his Atlanta Hawks teammate and defending dunk contest champion Dominique Wilkins.

Though he had a well-rounded game, Spud Webb was best known for his ability to dunk the ball.

Hawks
4

The acrobatic Wilkins towered more than a foot taller than Webb.

But the tiny guard would not be deterred. Over and over, Webb soared toward the basket and made magic happen in midair. On one dunk he spun his body completely around before slamming the ball through the hoop. Another time he did a double pump, then finished with a two-handed slam.

Webb then showed off his 42-inch vertical leap to cap his performance. He bounced the ball off the floor and the backboard, grabbed it with one hand, and jammed it through

Webb broke through on the national stage while playing for North Carolina State.

the hoop. The crowd went wild. He received a perfect score. Webb was the dunking champion of the world.

He was proud of his achievement. But he was used to accomplishing big things with his small body in a sport of giants.

Anthony "Spud" Webb was born in Dallas in 1963. As a kid he dreamed of playing in the NBA. But his size proved to be an obstacle along the way. He tried out for his high school team but was put on the junior varsity because he was too small. Rather than quit, he practiced harder. Finally given a chance on varsity, he led the team to the playoffs. He averaged 26 points per game and earned all-state honors as a senior.

That didn't convince major college programs to recruit Webb. He instead attended Midland Junior College and led the team to the junior college national title in 1982. That finally alerted the big schools to his talent. Webb landed at North Carolina State, where he averaged 10 points, six assists, and two steals a game in two seasons.

PAVING A PATH

Spud Webb's success gave other short players chances to compete in the NBA. Among them were 5-foot-3 Muggsy Bogues and 5-foot-5 Earl Boykins. Another was 5-foot-9 Nate Robinson, a three-time NBA Slam Dunk Contest winner. Twenty years after Webb won his title, Robinson leaped over Webb for the winning dunk.

That was enough to impress NBA scouts. The Detroit Pistons selected Webb in the fourth round of the 1985 NBA draft. However, he was cut during training camp. Fortunately, he earned a tryout with the Hawks. The rest is history.

Webb earned playing time right away and became a starter in 1986. He averaged 13 points and six assists per game with the Hawks and Sacramento Kings during the next five years. He proved unafraid of driving to the basket against the biggest and strongest players in the league. If he got knocked down, he would get up and attack the basket again. He understood the value of being resilient.

Spud Webb is a small man with a big heart. And that made him one of the greatest underdogs in NBA history.

Webb was used to taking on much taller players, including Boston Celtics great Larry Bird, *left*.

CHAPTER 3

GOLDEN NUGGETS

Football coaches like to say that defense wins championships. The same can be true in the NBA. Just ask the 1993–94 Denver Nuggets.

The Nuggets crawled into playoffs that season as the eighth seed. They had barely squeaked through with a 42–40 record. Their first-round opponent, the Seattle SuperSonics, had posted the best record in the league at 63–19. It looked like the Sonics would steamroll past Denver.

This fan predicted the Sonics would sweep Denver in the first round of the 1994 NBA playoffs.

13-0
SONICS

Dikembe Mutombo's shot-blocking skills were on display throughout the series.

Dikembe Mutombo had other plans. The Nuggets' 7-foot-2 center protected the hoop on defense. And he did not like intruders. Those who drove to the basket against Mutombo often had their shots rejected. Already one of the greatest defensive players in history, he averaged a league-best 4.1 blocked shots per game that season.

But that statistic was dwarfed by what he accomplished against Seattle.

The Sonics easily defeated the visiting Nuggets in the first two games, leaving them just one win away from a victory in the best-of-five series. An eighth seed had never defeated a top seed in the NBA playoffs. It seemed impossible for Denver to become the first by beating Seattle three games in a row.

But when the series switched to Denver, Mutombo embarked on a shot-blocking frenzy. He led the host Nuggets to lopsided victories in Games 3 and 4. Mutombo

THE FAMOUS FINGER WAG

Mutombo often wagged his finger at opponents after blocking their shots. It was his way of telling shooters not to test him. Early in his career, he would simply shake his head after swatting one away. The Hall of Famer added the finger-wag to warn shooters of his defensive dominance.

blocked 14 shots and grabbed 29 rebounds in those two wins. And his best was yet to come.

The Sonics remained heavily favored to win the series. After all, they had won 19 of their last 20 regular-season home games. The Nuggets had played four games in Seattle that year, including two in the playoffs, and had lost all four of them—by an average of 20 points.

Even Denver coach Dan Issel seemed resigned to the probability of defeat. Before Game 5 he spoke about accomplishing the goal of getting his young players some playoff experience. A series victory didn't seem to be in the cards.

Game 5 might have been played on Seattle's court, but the lane belonged to Mutombo. He refused to allow the Sonics easy looks at the basket. He blocked eight shots and hauled down 15 rebounds as Denver won in overtime. Mutombo received offensive support from teammates Robert Pack and LaPhonso Ellis. Brian Williams contributed 17 points and 19 rebounds in a stunning 98–94 victory that catapulted Denver into the second round.

When it was all over and Mutombo had grabbed the last rebound, his teammates piled on top of him in celebration. They knew that they had made history. And though they lost their second-round series to the Utah Jazz, nobody would forget Mutombo's amazing effort.

Mutombo still appears to be stunned as he walks off the floor after the Nuggets completed their huge upset.

CHAPTER 4

DYNAMITE DEFENDER

Most NBA stars come to the league from college powerhouses. They played at basketball factories such as Duke, North Carolina, Kansas, or Kentucky.

Not Ben Wallace. He spent two years at Cuyahoga Community College in Cleveland. He then finished up at Division II Virginia Union. Neither program was even a blip on the NBA radar, but Wallace made his presence known once he reached the pros.

Ben Wallace averaged 11.1 rebounds per game in his nine years with the Detroit Pistons.

SPALDING
NBA
PISTONS
3

Wallace, *right*, was never afraid of mixing it up under the basket.

Growing up in rural Alabama, Wallace had yearned to leap like Michael Jordan and shoot like Larry Bird. He eventually realized that he could only maximize his talent through hard work. Such attributes had been instilled in him by his mother, who insisted her son help the family by mowing grass and baling hay. Young Ben emerged as an all-state athlete in football, basketball, and baseball. But he was largely ignored by basketball scouts.

Wallace found a great teacher. He attended a camp run by New York Knicks star Charles Oakley, another big man whose NBA career centered on defense. Oakley urged him to hone his talents at Cuyahoga, where Wallace averaged 24 points and 17 rebounds per game as a sophomore. Then in 1994 he transferred to Virginia Union, where Oakley also played his college ball. Wallace led that team to the Division II Final Four.

ANOTHER FINE WALLACE

Wallace was not the only hard-working defender on the 2004 NBA champion Pistons. He wasn't even the only hard-working defender named Wallace. The other was Rasheed Wallace, a four-time All-Star who averaged a career-high 2.0 blocked shots per game for Detroit that season.

Even that did not motivate NBA teams to draft him. When Wallace failed in tryouts with the Boston Celtics and an Italian professional team, he gave up on basketball, opting for law school instead. But when the Washington Bullets invited him for a workout in 1996, he jumped at the offer. Wallace earned the last spot on Washington's roster. He barely played but did stay on the team all year. The coaches loved how hard he worked in practice.

The Orlando Magic traded for Wallace in 1999. He started all but one game that year for the Magic despite averaging just 4.8 points per game. He emerged as a dedicated defender. He led the team in rebounding and finished second

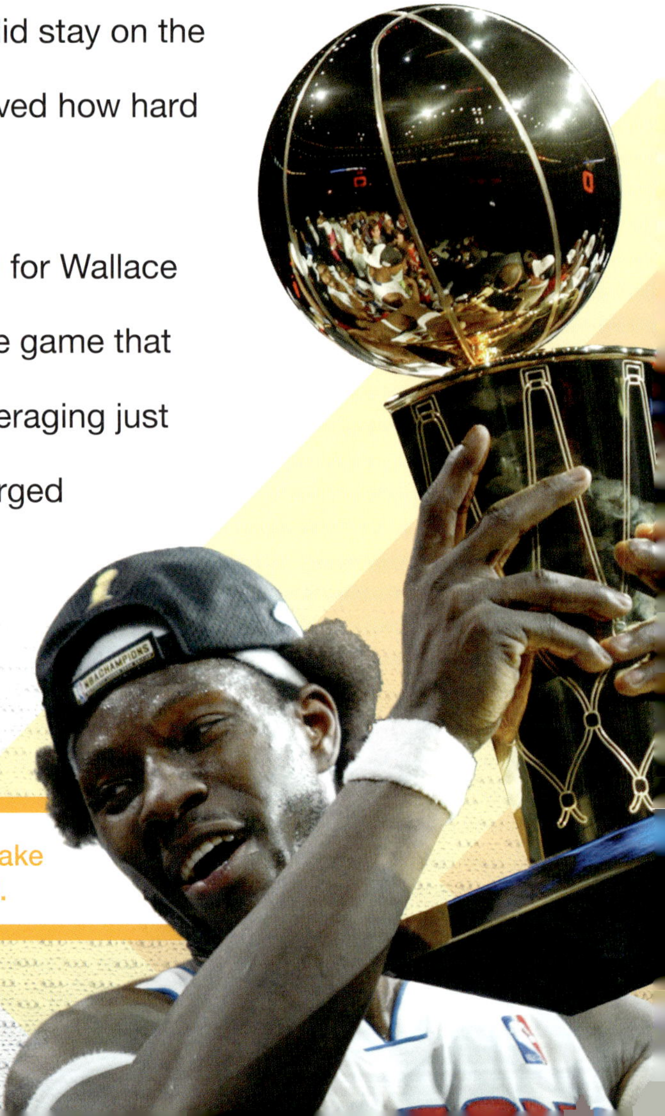

Wallace's hard work helped make him an NBA champion in 2004.

in blocked shots. He then landed in Detroit, where he blossomed into a star.

Nobody expected such progress. But Wallace had what many others did not—a passion for defense. He developed into the premier defender in the NBA. He won Defensive Player of the Year honors four times in five seasons.

Wallace also helped the Pistons win the NBA title in 2004. His defense helped control Los Angeles Lakers superstar Shaquille O'Neal in the Finals.

Wallace never averaged more than 9.7 points per game in an NBA season. Yet he turned his defensive skills and intensity into a long and successful career. By the time he retired in 2012, he had spent 16 seasons in the NBA, nearly all of them as a full-time starter.

Whether Wallace was the best undrafted player in NBA history is up for debate. But he certainly put up a great argument. And he proved that there is always a roster spot for a defender that plays with passion.

CHAPTER 5

WARRIOR WIPEOUT

The Golden State Warriors were considered doomed as their 2007 first-round playoff matchup against the top-seeded Dallas Mavericks approached. The Warriors had barely snuck into the playoffs with a record of 42–40. It was their first postseason appearance in 13 years. And none of their players had earned a spot on the Western Conference All-Star team.

Meanwhile, the Mavericks boasted the best record in the NBA at 67–15. Dallas also had one of the top weapons

Jason Richardson and the Warriors were primed to pull off a huge upset against Dallas.

SPALDING
WARRIORS
23

in the sport: forward Dirk Nowitzki, a deadly outside shooter who also could dominate close to the basket.

Never mind that Golden State won all three meetings against the Mavericks in the regular season. Dallas was

Dirk Nowitzki, *left*, and the Mavericks had no answer for Baron Davis.

the clear favorite in the best-of-seven series. Few gave the Warriors a chance. After all, they had surrendered the most points in the NBA that year. And Dallas was among the premier defensive teams in the league, so it would be difficult for the Warriors to try to outscore the Mavs.

But the Warriors did have one important ingredient to success—confidence. They also featured a talented guard in Baron Davis. Davis ran hot-and-cold with his offensive game. And in this series, he caught fire. Nowitzki was a future Hall of Famer. But Davis was easily the best player in the series.

HOPPING ON BOARD

The playoff success of the 2007 Warriors caught the attention of many celebrities. Among those who attended Game 6 to watch them clinch the upset were rapper Snoop Dogg, actress Kate Hudson, and legendary rock star Carlos Santana.

He wasted no time proving it, scoring 33 points in Game 1 while Nowitzki hit just 4 of 16 shots in a stunning blowout.

The first chapter of one of the greatest underdog stories in NBA history had been written. The Warriors won Games 3 and 4 at home, with Davis again scoring 33 points in Game 4 to give his team a 3–1 lead in the series. The Mavericks survived Game 5 back in Dallas, but Golden State had a chance to put them away at home two nights later.

It was no contest. The Warriors polished off the No. 1 seed with a 111–86 blowout. The Warriors led just 50–48 at halftime, but they outscored Dallas by 21 points in the third quarter to put it away. And though Davis scored 20 points in the clincher, backcourt mate Stephen Jackson played the role of hero. He hit an amazing 7 of 8 three-point attempts to finish with 33 points.

Davis averaged 25 points per game and hit 54 percent of his shots in the series. He did receive plenty of help

Nowitzki's face says it all as the Mavericks slink off the court after getting knocked out of the playoffs.

from Jackson and Jason Richardson, both of whom could play guard or small forward. Jackson chipped in 22.8 points per game, while Richardson added 19.5.

When it was over, Richardson could hardly contain his excitement. "This is everything I wanted," he said. "I wanted this for our fans, for our organization, for ourselves. We work hard, and we deserve it."

CHAPTER 6

OUT OF NOWHERE

The New York Knicks were a mess. It was early February 2012 and their record was a dismal 8–15. They had lost 11 of their previous 13 games. The Knicks needed a spark.

Nobody expected it to come from an unknown guard named Jeremy Lin. Up to that point, Lin had been a fringe player, at best, in the NBA. He had spent a short time with Golden State and was barely hanging onto his roster spot at the end of the bench for the Knicks.

Jeremy Lin starred at Harvard, a school not known for producing NBA prospects.

HARVAR
4

Lin was the unlikeliest of basketball stars. He stood just 5 feet 3 inches tall as a freshman in high school. Lin's father had immigrated from Taiwan. No Taiwanese-American had ever worn an NBA uniform. Lin also had played at Harvard University. No one from that school had made it to the NBA in almost 50 years.

Once he got a chance to play in New York, Lin seemed to be everywhere on the court.

The path to the NBA had been a tough one for Lin, even after he grew 12 inches during high school. He was taunted from the stands during high school games. Hecklers screamed that he belonged on the math team or in the orchestra rather than the basketball court. Others even shouted racial slurs.

Lin had not been given a chance to show his talents with the Knicks when the team was struggling. Desperate and seemingly out of options, coach Mike D'Antoni finally gave him a shot.

That's how "Linsanity" was born. Lin immediately rattled off a string of eye-popping performances. He scored 25 points and added seven assists against the Nets. He posted 28 points and eight assists against Utah. He recorded 23 points and 10 assists against Washington. He exploded for 38 points and seven assists against the Lakers.

His average of 27.2 points was the highest of any NBA player in his first five games since 1976. The Knicks won all of them to launch a seven-game winning streak. Lin remained in the starting lineup and became a fan favorite.

Lin was gaining fame. And the greatest guard in Knicks history, Hall of Famer Walt Frazier, praised Lin for his all-around talent.

"(Lin) does what needs to be done," Frazier said. "If they need scoring, he provides that. He's very unselfish, once he gets inside he's looking to pass

Lin went on to a successful career that included stints with a number of NBA teams, including the Houston Rockets.

the ball. But when there's an opportunity to let him score, he's doing that as well. He's just unflappable."

A knee injury ended his season early, but a free-agent offer from Houston the following year gave him a new opportunity. He landed a job as a full-time starter for the Rockets, averaging 13.4 points and 6.1 assists per game.

Lin went on to play for the Los Angeles Lakers, Charlotte Hornets, and Brooklyn Nets, and he signed with the Atlanta Hawks in 2018. He never again reached the greatness that he displayed briefly for the Knicks. But he had proven that even the ultimate underdog can star in the NBA if given the chance.

THE RESULT OF LINSANITY

The price of Knicks tickets skyrocketed due to Linsanity. One ticket for a game against New Orleans sold for nearly $4,000. The minimum price was $183. Before Lin arrived on the scene, tickets were available for as low as $47.

CHAPTER 7

BLOSSOMING BULL

Jimmy Butler was not just an underdog as a basketball player. He was an underdog in life. And his achievements off the court make his achievements on the court seem even more incredible.

It all began in the small town of Tomball, Texas. Butler's dad abandoned the family when he was a baby. Jimmy and his mother clashed so badly that she threw him out of the house at age 13. He was homeless until he moved in with the family of a high school teammate.

Jimmy Butler (33) worked hard to earn playing time at Marquette.

AL
MARQUETTE
33
PIRATES
BIG EAST
MITCHELL
23

Butler, *left*, became an All-Star in Chicago.

Basketball seemed unlikely to save him. Butler attracted little attention from major college scouts despite having proven himself the best player on his team. He played one season at Tyler Junior College before a high school teammate recommended him to Marquette University coach Buzz Williams.

Williams took the tough approach on Butler. "I was brutal because I wanted him to make it." Williams said. "He was weak, he was overwhelmed, but he never quit. Jimmy just kept showing up."

Butler earned a starting spot by his junior season. He averaged 15 points a game over the next two years while excelling defensively. His toughness piqued the interest of Chicago's defensive-minded coach Tom Thibodeau. The Bulls selected Butler with the 30th overall choice in the 2011 NBA draft. Fans criticized the pick. They wanted their team to take a more explosive scorer.

A BUDDY FOR BUTLER

One of Butler's best friends is actor Mark Wahlberg. The two met when Wahlberg was in Chicago in 2013 filming a *Transformers* movie. He dropped by the Bulls' training facility looking to shoot some hoops. Butler complied and the two struck up a lasting friendship.

Little did they know that Butler had plenty of offensive talent hidden inside him. He didn't even realize it himself. He certainly could not have imagined blossoming into a great scorer after averaging just 2.6 points a game in limited playing time as a rookie. But the work ethic that would define his career did not allow him to stagnate.

Butler soon proved to be the biggest bargain in basketball. He toiled tirelessly on his shooting stroke. He scored 20 points a game during the 2014–15 season. He became a deadly long-distance marksman, hitting 38 percent of his three-point attempts. He won the NBA Most Improved Player Award in 2015. Yet he was one of the lowest-paid players on his team.

Not for long. The Bulls had offered him a four-year, $44 million contract before that season. But Butler turned it down. He had supreme confidence in himself. He believed he could earn more if he performed well. And he was right. He signed a five-year, $95 million deal in July 2015.

Butler spent two more seasons with Chicago and averaged a career-high 23.9 points per game in the 2016–17 season. He was then traded to the Minnesota Timberwolves, where he was reunited with Thibodeau. His talent and experience helped that young team into the playoffs for the first time in 14 years. He recorded career-bests in shooting percentage and steals for the Wolves.

Butler had become a four-time All-Star and an Olympic gold medal winner who earned spots on four NBA All-Defensive teams. Not bad for someone who went unnoticed by major college programs when he came out of high school.

Butler was part of Team USA at the 2016 Rio Olympics.

GLOSSARY

assist

A pass that leads directly to a basket.

contract

An agreement to play for a certain team.

draft

A system that allows teams to acquire new players coming into a league.

immigrate

To move from one country to another.

scholarship

Money awarded to a student-athlete to pay for education expenses.

scout

A person whose job is to look for talented young players.

seed

The ranking assigned to a team playing in a tournament.

stutter

Talk with continued involuntary repetition of sounds, especially initial consonants.

therapy

Treatment intended to relieve or heal a disorder.

MORE INFORMATION

BOOKS

Bryant, Howard. *Legends: The Best Players, Games, and Teams in Basketball*. New York: Philomel Books, 2013.

Gitlin, Marty. *NBA's Top 10 Playoff Upsets*. Minneapolis, MN: Abdo Publishing, 2019.

Sports Illustrated Kids. *Big Book of WHO Basketball*. New York: Sports Illustrated Kids, 2015.

ONLINE RESOURCES

Booklinks
NONFICTION NETWORK
FREE! ONLINE NONFICTION RESOURCES

To learn more about basketball underdogs, visit abdobooklinks.com. These links are routinely monitored and updated to provide the most current information available.

INDEX

ABOUT THE AUTHOR

Marty Gitlin is a freelance educational book author based in Cleveland, Ohio. He has had more than 140 books published, many in the realm of sports. He also won more than 45 awards as a newspaper sportswriter from 1991 to 2002. Included was a first place for general excellence from Associated Press in 1996. That organization also selected him as one of the top four feature writers in Ohio.